MONTANA
Moments

PHOTOGRAPHY BY CHUCK HANEY

FARCOUNTRY
PRESS

RIGHT: Upper Missouri River Breaks National Monument encompasses nearly 600 square miles of prairie, forests, and badlands. This formation, called a hoodoo, was formed by eons of wind and rain eroding the softer layers under a hard caprock.

TITLE PAGE: A banner year for beargrass blossoms, seen here above Grinnell Lake in Glacier National Park. Bears carry mouthfuls of the fibrous grassy leaves to create a soft bed in their winter dens.

COVER: The Dearborn River sculpted Devil's Glen, protected today as part of the Scapegoat Wilderness. Lewis and Clark named the river for Henry Dearborn, the secretary of war for President Thomas Jefferson.

BACK COVER: Wild iris, also called blue flag, carpets the prairie grasslands along the Rocky Mountain Front near Choteau. A few miles from Choteau, the discovery of a fossilized nest of duck-billed dinosaur eggs and young rocked the paleontological world by revealing that some dinosaurs tended their broods.

FLAP, TOP: Sinopah Mountain's "Diving Board" provides a perfect view of Two Medicine Lake in Glacier National Park. The Blackfoot name for Two Medicine is *Natoki-Okas. Oka* means to sleep and hints of tribal use of the area for vision quests.

FLAP, BOTTOM: Jerusalem Rocks glow in the winter light, near Montana's northern border town of Sweet Grass. These rocks reach 3,576 feet in elevation and are accessible only by hiking.

BELOW: Bighorn sheep find safe refuge atop the steep cliffs in the Upper Missouri River Breaks National Monument.

ISBN 13: 978-1-56037-703-0

© 2018 by Farcountry Press
Photography © 2018 by Chuck Haney

For more information about our books, write Farcountry Press, P.O. Box 5630, Helena, MT 59604; call (800) 821-3874; or visit www.farcountrypress.com.

Produced in the United States.
Printed in China.

23 22 21 20 19 18   1 2 3 4 5 6

FOREWORD

by Chuck Haney

I have had the good fortune to spend almost three decades being a proud Montanan. *Montana Moments* marks my fourth photography book highlighting landscapes across the state that I truly love. There is a diverse and endless supply of flowing rivers, tranquil lakes, high mountain peaks, and miles upon miles of rolling prairie landscapes to keep any photographer happy. Montana flows with life: abundant wildlife roams the forests, prairie skies fill with birds, and waters teem with fish.

One of the most satisfying aspects of my constant exploration of the state has been capturing the spirit of

passion for living a robust life in Montana.

I would like to thank my family for all the support they have given me in the past several decades while I spent countless hours tucked away in some remote corner of the state waiting for just the perfect light.

I look forward to the next chapter of my life and exploring much more of my home state. Montana always delivers those special moments.

its residents being drawn to life as it unfolds in front of my lenses. I value the friendships made with numerous ranchers and farmers. Each spring I can't wait to witness small-town Montana come to life at the high school basketball tournament, after photographing historical architecture in Uptown Butte. Before heading back home, I stop and listen in awe as upwards of 100,000 snow geese take off en masse at Freezeout Lake. Each summer I appreciate and learn more about Native American culture at the North American Indian Days while taking portraits or capturing fast-charging rodeo action.

Unique events like listening to legendary "Piano Pat" Spoonheim while mermaids swim at the Sip 'n Dip in Great Falls or visiting a ferry operator to cross a remote section of the Missouri River are true Montana moments.

I cherish documenting my adventures with friends as we mountain bike, hike, paddle, fish, and ski to celebrate our

ABOVE: "Piano Pat" Spoonheim plays as a "mermaid" swims in a tank at the Sip 'n Dip Tiki Lounge in Great Falls. Pat's memory for lyrics and accompaniment is legendary.

TOP: Main Street in Uptown Butte seems designed to direct your eyes to admire the nearby snow-covered Continental Divide. Butte was known as "The Richest Hill on Earth" for the massive amounts of copper, gold, and silver mined there. In the 1890s it produced fully half the nation's copper.

LEFT: The Indian Relay Race inspires stiff competition during North American Indian Days in Browning. This is one of the biggest events for U.S. and Canadian tribes, who gather to celebrate the traditional native way of life. The pow wow and traditional games attract hundreds of competitors.

FACING PAGE: Three Bears Lake reflects Elk Mountain, at Marias Pass. The Great Northern Railway built their tracks across this pass in 1890–91, heavily promoting tourism that eventually resulted in the designation of Glacier National Park.

ABOVE: A short-eared owl keeps a keen eye out for small mammals and birds. Unlike many owl species, these owls hunt primarily during daylight.

RIGHT: Jewel Basin is a popular 15,349-acre hiker-only area that contains twenty-seven lakes and an uncountable number of graceful wildflowers. The basin lies on the west-facing slope of the Swan Range and provides mighty views across the Flathead Valley.

NEXT PAGES: Sweethearts enjoy the last moments of daylight from the city beach and dock on Whitefish Lake.

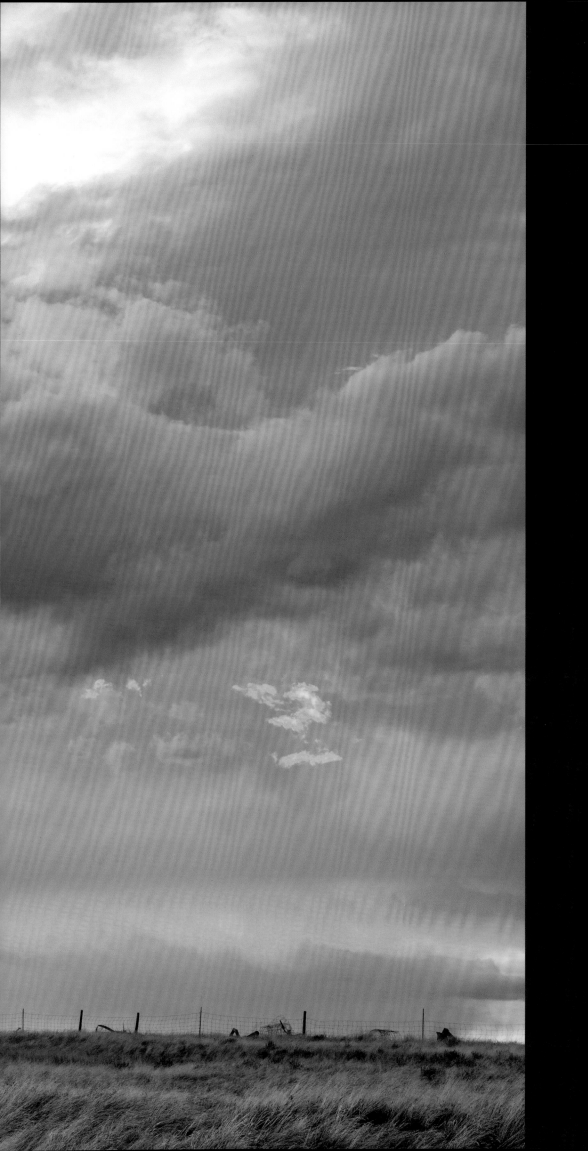

ABOVE: Mountain bluebird males are among the first songbirds to return to Montana in the spring. Pairs nest in tree cavities or dirt banks, or readily move into human-made nesting boxes. In a good year, they may raise two broods before departing for milder climes.

LEFT: Wooden granaries were ubiquitous in early-day Montana, but they are now increasingly rare. This old granary near Choteau likely housed wheat, oats, or barley.

ABOVE: *The Riders of the Purple Sage* statue overlooks the Missouri River trail in downtown Fort Benton. This community was the terminus for riverboats bringing people and supplies up the Missouri during the heyday of Montana's gold rush in the 1860s and 1870s.

RIGHT: The lush habitat seen here is created by a backwater, or slough, of the Flathead River. The Flathead watershed sustains more than 300 species of aquatic insects, nearly half of them stoneflies. Stoneflies spend their first years on the bottom of rivers; the well-camouflaged nymphs hide under river stones.

BELOW: Reminder of mortality: a cow skull rests amid prairie wildflowers in the 59,000-acre Bitter Creek Wilderness Study Area near Hinsdale. This scenic area is popular with hikers, hunters, and wildlife watchers.

ABOVE: The Silver Gate General Store serves the hamlet of Silver Gate (population 140, elevation 7,600 feet), one mile east of the Northeast Entrance Station for Yellowstone National Park. Silver Gate enjoys nearly 200 inches of snowfall each winter.

LEFT: A mature bull elk can weigh up to 1,000 pounds. They summer at high elevations, but move downhill in winter to forage on grass and shrubs.

FAR LEFT: On its way through Gallatin Canyon about eighteen miles south of Four Corners, U.S. Highway 191 affords views of craggy 7,165-foot Storm Castle Peak and the always-scenic Gallatin River.

RIGHT: Sunset colors the sky and the rocks at Medicine Rocks State Park, near Ekalaka. The soft sandstone has eroded into pocked formations that invite close examination. Sit quietly, and you might spot a Woodhouse's toad or a sharp-tailed grouse nearby.

BELOW: This pretty, drought-tolerant wildflower called Miner's Candle catches the light in the sun-drenched prairie near Dupuyer along the Rocky Mountain Front. More than 2,500 species of vascular plants grow in Montana.

ABOVE: West Shore State Park abuts the rocky shoreline of Flathead Lake near Lakeside. People come here to camp, picnic, fish, and swim. Montana has fifty-four diverse state parks that span the state, ranging from historical sites to geological wonders to swimming holes.

LEFT: Flathead Lake, the largest natural freshwater lake west of the Mississippi, creates its own microclimate that permits sweet cherry trees and even peach trees to thrive—nearly unheard of anywhere else in the state.

NEXT PAGES: Wheat is Montana's leading cash crop, seen here growing in view of the Tobacco Root Mountains near Ennis. The state is renowned for its excellent hard red winter wheat, hard red spring wheat, and durum wheat. Montana exports 80 percent of its wheat crop to eager buyers around the world.

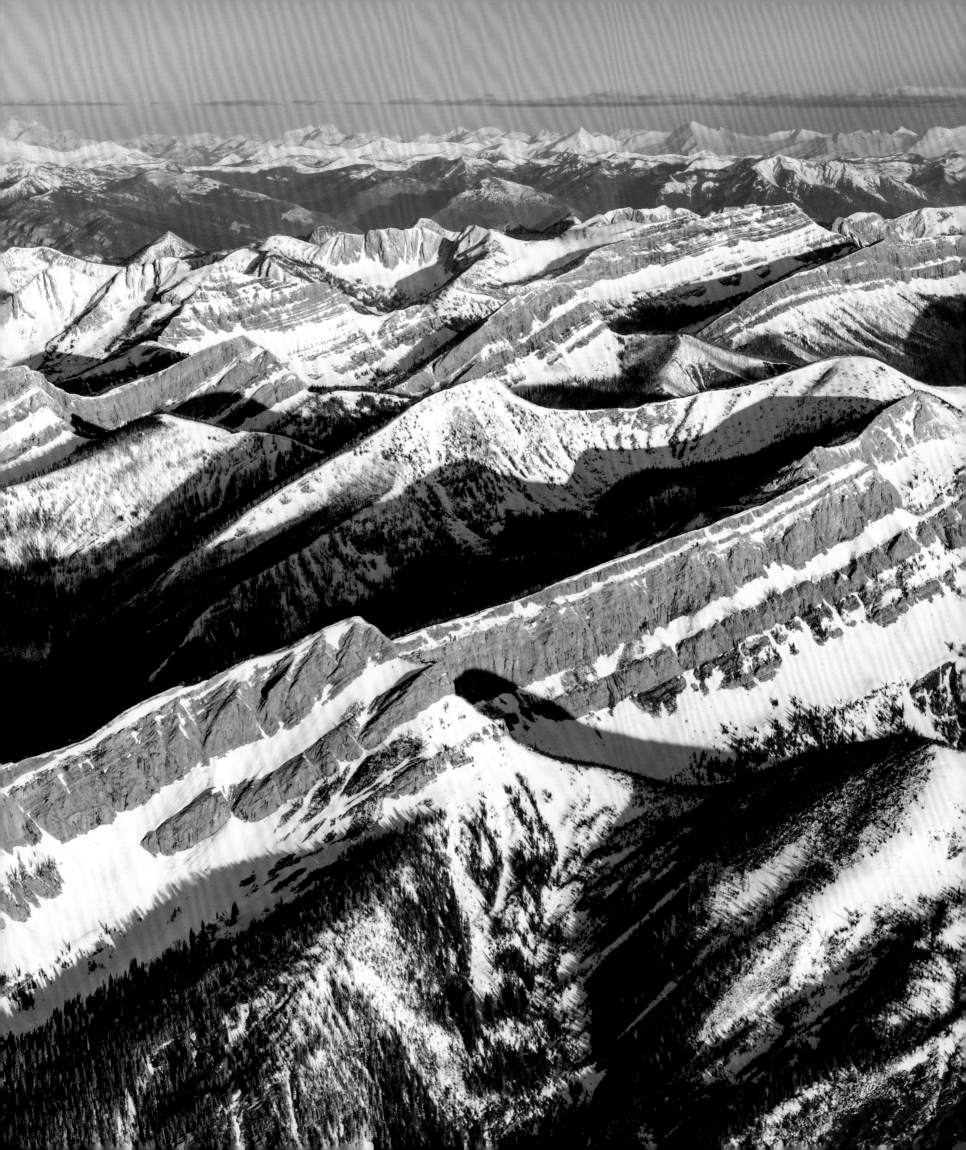

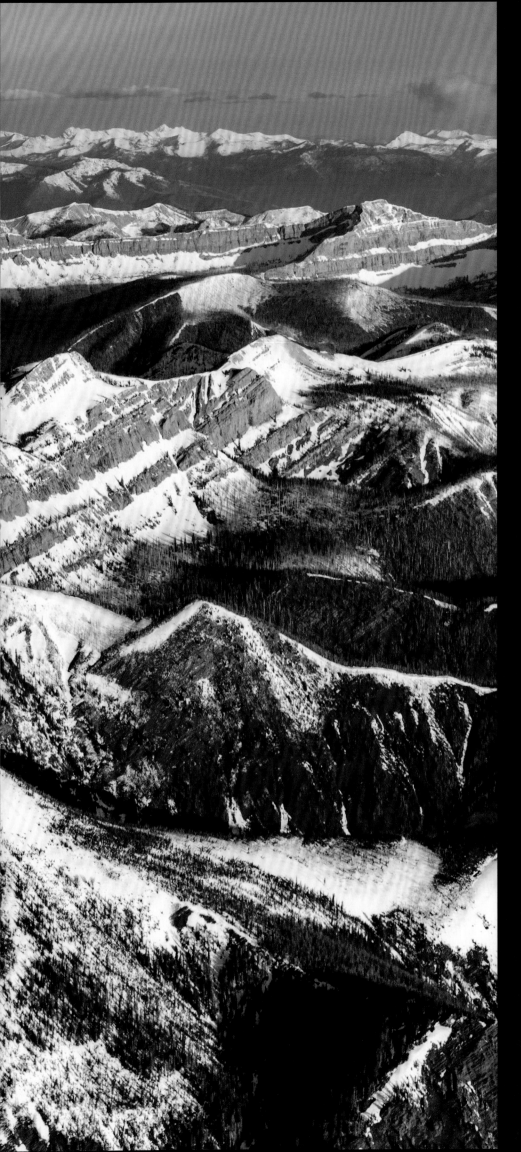

LEFT: The Bob Marshall Wilderness, established in 1964, encompasses more than a million acres of rugged topography that shelters top predators, including grizzlies, wolves, lynx, and wolverines. Together with the adjacent Great Bear Wilderness to the north and the Scapegoat Wilderness to the south, this is the third-largest wilderness in the lower 48 states.

BELOW: In addition to traditional dogsledding, the annual Flathead Classic dogsled race features the entertaining—and precarious—"skijoring," when a person on skis is pulled by dogs or a horse.

ABOVE: The meltwaters of Sexton Glacier feed Baring Creek, which scoured out the magnificent Sunrift Gorge in Glacier National Park. This unique and colorful gorge is viewable by taking a short hike from the park's Going-to-the-Sun Road.

RIGHT: Rays of sun penetrate the forest floor at Ross Creek Cedars Scenic Area, in the Kootenai National Forest. These protected old-growth western redcedars grow to 175 feet tall and 12 feet in diameter.

LEFT: Morning sunlight illuminates Square Butte near Great Falls. Charles M. Russell featured this recognizable landmark in several of his paintings, such as his well-known *Charles M. Russell and His Friends*.

BELOW: A tom turkey struts his breeding plumage in spring, hoping to attract a mate. Montana is home to wild Merriam's turkeys and other upland game birds such as pheasants, grouse, partridges, and chukars.

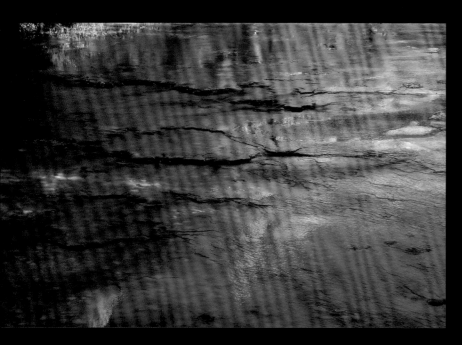

ABOVE: Autumn reflections enhance the tranquil beauty of a creek in the Swan Valley. This valley holds more surface water than any other watershed in Montana; a 1,300-mile network of streams carries water throughout the valley.

RIGHT: Time-lapse photography created this composite image of stars over the peaks that surround Lake McDonald in Glacier National Park.

BELOW: Lewis and Clark Caverns was Montana's first state park. Visitors can tour the limestone caverns to see stalactites, stalagmites, and other fabulous formations created by eons of dripping water.

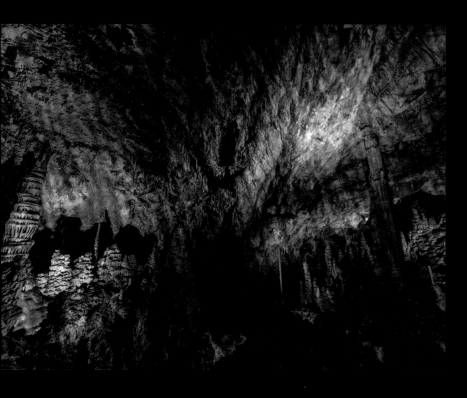

LEFT: Spanish Creek threads a meadow below the Spanish Peaks in the north end of the Madison Range west of Bozeman.

BELOW: Moose can close their nostrils in order to forage underwater on water-loving plants. These large mammals weigh up to 1,200 pounds and can swim for miles, even diving to get at plants that grow in deep water.

ABOVE: Werner Peak provides a perfect viewpoint to admire a stormy sunset in the Stillwater State Forest. The Stillwater is Montana's oldest state forest, and at 93,000 acres it also is the largest.

RIGHT: A rainbow signifies the end of rain showers over Widgeon Pond in Red Rock Lakes National Wildlife Refuge. The refuge is best known for its population of trumpeter swans, the largest swan in the world.

NEXT PAGES: Makoshika State Park preserves and protects 11,538 acres of badlands and dinosaur fossils in eastern Montana. It is Montana's largest state park, with camping, an excellent interpretive center, dinosaur fossils, and miles of hiking trails.

BELOW: Shooting star blossoms can carpet the prairie in early spring, turning an entire field pink. One plant can produce as many as a dozen delicate blooms.

ABOVE: A male lazuli bunting sings a warning to potential competitors at the National Bison Range near Moiese. The brightly colored males are easy to spot as they sing in the open, but the brown females are more reclusive.

LEFT: A favorite of travelers for more than a century, Granite Park Chalet in Glacier National Park sits above it all at 6,500 feet. The rustic chalet, built by the Great Northern Railway in 1914, provides a welcome respite after the 7.6-mile hike from Logan Pass.

BELOW: The turquoise water of Medicine Grizzly Lake is just one of the spectacular features seen by those who hike the Triple Divide Pass Trail in Glacier National Park. Scientists use DNA analysis and radio collaring to estimate that the park shelters about 300 grizzly bears and 600 black bears.

ABOVE: A climber tackles a wall at the Stone Hill climbing area, along Lake Koocanusa. This reservoir was named for three adjacent places: the Kootenai River, Canada, and the USA.

RIGHT: The sun burnishes a small butte above the South Fork of the Judith River in the Little Belt Mountains northeast of White Sulphur Springs.

BELOW: Pikas gather forbs and grasses to dry in the sun before taking them into their rock dens to feed on throughout the winter. Deep snow above their dens serves as an insulating blanket.

LEFT: Wolves were reintroduced to Yellowstone in 1995 amid much controversy. The predator-prey balance in the park soon shifted and the effects rippled outward. For instance, elk stopped spending long periods of time in the river bottoms, and beavers, willows, and aspens subsequently increased and now thrive.

FAR LEFT: Palisade Falls pours over the columnar basalt in Hyalite Canyon south of Bozeman. The name comes from the glass-like hyalite crystals found at the base of Hyalite Peak.

BELOW: Bison are the largest land animals in North America, with adult males reaching 2,000 pounds. In Montana, bison are found near Yellowstone National Park and at the National Bison Range near St. Ignatius.

ABOVE: A juvenile red-tailed hawk shows its incredible athleticism while launching from its perch. Red-tailed hawks are widespread throughout Montana and the nation. They hunt rodents, rabbits, small birds, snakes, and more.

RIGHT: The Big Hole River is one of Montana's revered trout fisheries, nurturing Arctic grayling, mountain whitefish, burbot, and several species of trout. About 450 miles of Montana's rivers are designated "blue-ribbon" trout fishing.

ABOVE: A prairie rain squall and low-angled sunlight create dramatic lighting near Lewistown.

LEFT: The sun peeks through snow ghosts at Whitefish Mountain Resort, which has 105 marked runs and four terrain parks on its 3,000 acres. The "fata morgana" in the background clouds is a mirage that looks like buttes and pinnacles.

RIGHT: Chokecherries bloom at Pictograph Cave State Park near Billings. In late summer, the mature cherries on this Montana native plant will feed numerous species of birds—and make a tasty jelly.

BELOW: Prehistoric hunters left behind more than 100 rock paintings, now protected at Pictograph Cave State Park. Some of the pictographs may be 2,000 years old. Evidence shows that generations of these early hunters took shelter in the three main caves.

ABOVE: Werner Peak Lookout glows with lantern light in the Stillwater State Forest. Even though the slow camera exposure makes it appear that the stars are moving, you are actually seeing the result of the Earth's rotation.

LEFT: The aurora borealis lends a mystical quality to a stylized tepee sculpture near St. Mary on the Blackfeet Indian Reservation. The reservation encompasses about 1.5 million acres and is governed by the Blackfeet Tribal Business Council.

BELOW: There are few things more wonderful than lying on your back in the Kootenai National Forest, gazing at the night sky full of stars. This national forest, established in 1907, spans 2.2 million acres of natural resources in Montana's northwestern corner.

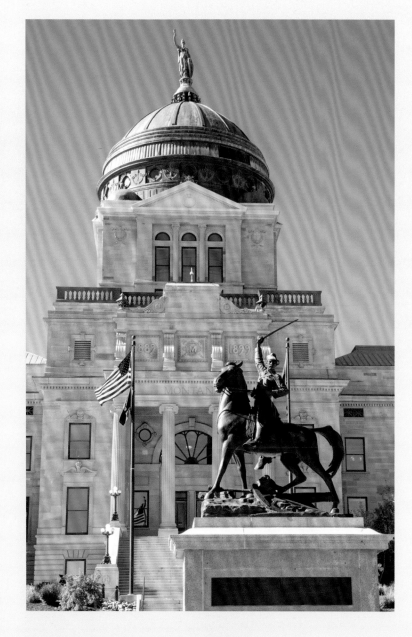

ABOVE: The Montana State Capitol in Helena is guarded by a statue of Thomas Meagher, acting governor of Montana Territory after the Civil War. Construction on the capitol began in 1899, and the massive sandstone and granite structure was completed in 1912.

RIGHT: Helena's South Hills provide panoramic views of the Helena Valley, also known as the Valley of the Prickly Pear for the cactus that grows there. The iconic silhouette of the prone Sleeping Giant adorns the horizon.

ABOVE: A perfectly ripe huckleberry: delicious! Montana's "hucks" grow in habitats from 2,000 feet to above 11,000 feet in elevation, but they stubbornly refuse to be domesticated—you simply have to get out into the wild country to find them.

LEFT: Hell Roaring Creek, along with Swift Creek and Lazy Creek, flows into Whitefish Lake—a 7-mile-long pristine lake popular for outdoor recreation. Autumn brings crisp, cool mornings and splashes of brillant color from the many deciduous trees and shrubs in the area.

BELOW: Grizzly bears feed on vegetation and insects 90 percent of the time, searching out berries, roots, grasses, mushrooms, bugs, invertebrates, and fruit. They will also eat fish, carrion, and mammals when they can find them.

"Gallows" frames light up the night, commemorating the mining history of Butte. More than $48 billion of copper, gold, and silver were pried from the mines here. The Montana Bureau of Mines estimates there are 10,000 miles of mining tunnels with thousands of underground shafts.

ABOVE: Raccoons are year-round residents of Montana, favoring riparian and wetland habitats. They are omnivorous and smart, and will readily eat food left untended by humans.

LEFT: Lupine blooms along Jacobson Creek, a tributary of the Wise River in the East Pioneer Mountains. Many wild animals can consume silky lupine, and native peoples used the seeds to make an eye medicine.

BELOW: Sticky geranium are so named because their stems have a sticky feel. This hardy member of the rose family grows from the lower valleys to subalpine regions in western Montana.

ABOVE: Bald eagles build their nests near rivers and lakes, often returning to the same place year after year. This can result in gigantic nests, some as big as twelve feet tall and eight feet in diameter.

RIGHT: The Yellowstone River originates in Yellowstone Lake, then flows north past Emigrant Peak in the Paradise Valley before wending east to its eventual confluence with the Missouri River. Its 692 miles of untamed, undammed waters make the Yellowstone the nation's longest free-flowing river.

BELOW: A mule deer fawn stays close to its mother, alert to any motion or sound. Mule deer are year-round inhabitants of Montana, eating mostly forbs in summer and browsing on shrubs in winter.

ABOVE: In winter, snowy owls often venture across Montana's northern border from their normal range in Canada. These large owls hunt primarily for rodents but can also take rabbits and waterfowl.

LEFT: The train depot in Whitefish is still an active hub of transportation for Amtrak. The very first train rolled into Whitefish in 1904 when there was barely a town here; the Great Northern Railway built this attractive timber-frame, Tudor-style depot in 1924.

BELOW: The historic Izaak Walton Inn, in Essex, has renovated train cabooses into delightful lodging. The inn was built in 1939 for $40,000; it originally housed railroad workers but is now a popular destination for train buffs, cross-country skiers, and hikers.

ABOVE: Charolais cattle are bred for their meat. The breed, well adapted to Montana, originated in Burgundy, France. This cute little calf may grow to weigh one ton.

RIGHT: This beautifully tended farm along Indian Creek, near Eureka, has a perfect view of the Whitefish Range. The plentiful native whitefish gave their name to a town, a river, a lake, and a mountain range in Montana.

BELOW: Montana farmers harvest more than 50,000 tons of corn silage annually, seen here near Park City. Corn silage is used to feed cattle.

LEFT: Bighorn Canyon National Recreation Area provides a perfect view of the Bighorn River which carved—and is still carving—this canyon through thousands of feet of shale, sandstone, and limestone.

BELOW: The quiet currents of the broad Missouri River provide perfect canoeing alongside the White Cliffs in the Upper Missouri River Breaks National Monument. The 300-foot-high cliffs are formed of Eagle sandstone; the Lewis and Clark Expedition described this stretch of river as having "seens [sic] of visionary enchantment." Today's visitors can see petroglyphs, homestead buildings, and ancient tepee rings near the river.

ABOVE: A mountain goat male, called a billy, climbs across Altyn Ridge in Glacier National Park. Mature billies may reach 300 pounds, outweighing the nannies by 150 pounds.

RIGHT: Sunrise highlights Grinnell Point over Swiftcurrent Lake in Glacier National Park. The naturalist explorer George Bird Grinnell named the lake in the 1880s based on the Blackfoot name that means "swift flowing river."

BELOW: Looking like a necklace of jewels, bubbles from decaying vegetation form under the ice along the edge of Lake McDonald in Glacier National Park.

LEFT: Virgelle provides a perfect porch to ponder the eternal flows of the Missouri River, fondly called the Mighty Mo by locals. This tiny settlement is a popular boat launch for floating the Upper Missouri National Wild and Scenic River.

FACING PAGE: Rocky Valley Lutheran Church is the last building still standing in the ghost town of Dooley, near Plentywood in Montana's far northeastern corner. It was placed on the National Register of Historic Places in 1993.

NEXT PAGES: The lights of Florence provide a visual counter-balance to a lunar eclipse above Lolo Peak in the Bitterroot Mountains. Most years stargazers can see four lunar eclipses, but some years have up to seven.

BELOW: The elevators in Hingham stand ready to load their bushels of grain onto a train. The community was established in 1910 and within a year boasted a town square with twenty businesses.

ABOVE: Hell Creek State Park protects the wonderful and weirdly sculpted 65-million-year-old rocks of the Hell Creek Formation in Montana's sparsely populated Garfield County. Paleontologists have located fossilized remains of dinosaurs such as Tyrannosaurus and Triceratops, as well as invertebrates, plants, mammals, fish, reptiles, and amphibians.

LEFT: Native vegetation growing in the badlands near Fort Peck Reservoir has adapted to the extreme weather. It must green up quickly after a spring rain, then go back to its dormant golden color during the dry, hot summers and frigid winters, when the roots cannot get moisture from the soil.

ABOVE: Martin Falls cascades through the Flathead National Forest just before winter freeze-up. This 2.4-million-acre national forest borders Canada, encompassing wildernesses, lakes and rivers, and mountain ranges.

RIGHT: Sunrise reveals steam caused by the extreme temperature difference between the frigid air and the slightly warmer water of the South Fork of the Flathead River.

BELOW: Coyotes are one of nature's most adaptable animals, able to figure out how to live in Montana's deep winter snow as well as in desert canyons.

Encompassing more than 3,000-acres, Ninepipe Wildlife Management Area protects essential wetlands, ponds, and grassy upland benches that harbor shorebirds, waterfowl, and many species of songbirds. This unique habitat was created by retreating glaciers.

ABOVE: A kayaker braves a stormy autumn evening on Rainy Lake to get a perfect view of the Swan Range. The Swans stretch about 120 miles long and 66 miles wide, with peaks soaring to 9,000 feet and not a single road crossing the range.

RIGHT: Bicycle tourism in Montana is increasing every year as cyclists discover the miles and miles of lightly trafficked highways throughout the state.

LEFT: The Kootenai River is known for its blue-ribbon trout fishing. This lovely, modest-appearing waterway is the third-largest tributary, by volume, of the Columbia River.

RIGHT: In the foothills of the Little Snowy Range southeast of Lewistown, the protected Bear Gulch site holds more than 4,000 pictographs, perhaps the largest in *situ* collection of Plains Indian art in the United States.

FACING PAGE: A vast field of purple lupine leads your eye to the sinking sun, looking west from a hilltop above Missoula to the Bitterroot Mountains. The Salish harvested the roots of a nutritious, bitter plant in this valley, hence the name Bitterroot for the adjacent mountains, valley, and river.

BELOW: Now a state park fifteen miles northeast of Dillon, Beaverhead Rock was an important landmark for Shoshone and other tribes in the region. Sacagawea recognized the rock while traveling with Lewis and Clark in August of 1805 and knew her people, who would provide much-needed horses for the expedition, were nearby.

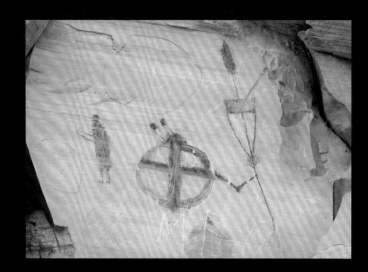

Terry Badlands Wilderness Study Area contains geological formations that look like spires, chimneys, tables, arches, and bridges. The badlands were formed by thousands of years of wind and water eroding the soft sedimentary rocks into deep gullies and fantastic shapes.

ABOVE: Near Springdale, the Yellowstone River winds through the valley greened by spring storms.

LEFT: Yellow-headed blackbirds prefer wetland habitat and build their cup-shaped nests over the water. The male's brilliant yellow head is unmistakable and his call is complex and varied.

FAR LEFT: The Madison River, seen here near Ennis, is a world-class fishery that might get you a trophy trout. Its headwaters originate in Yellowstone National Park and flow north before joining the Gallatin and Jefferson Rivers. These three rivers form the Missouri River.

ABOVE: Tepee poles stand as stark reminders of the Nez Perce who died in 1877 while trying to reach safe haven in Canada, memorialized here at Big Hole National Battlefield.

RIGHT: Headstones at Little Bighorn Battlefield National Monument commemorate Lt. Col. George Armstrong Custer's U.S. 7th Cavalry soldiers who were felled by Sioux, Northern Cheyenne, and Arapaho warriors in 1876.

BELOW: A colorfully clad youngster rides in the Crow Fair parade that kicks off one of the nation's largest pow wows, celebrated each year at Crow Agency.

ABOVE AND TOP: Pompeys Pillar rises 200 feet above the Yellowstone River east of Billings. William Clark carved his signature into the sandstone in 1806—the only remaining on-site physical evidence of the Lewis and Clark Expedition.

LEFT: A rocky outcrop overlooks the Little Bighorn River, seen here near Lodge Grass. This river originates in Wyoming and flows 138 miles north to its confluence with the Yellowstone River.

NEXT PAGES: Western larch turn golden before dropping their needles for the winter, seen here at peak color surrounding Holland Lake and climbing the lower slopes of the Mission Range. Western larch (*Larix occidentalis*) grows in Montana and the Pacific Northwest into Canada.

ABOVE: Big Sky Resort, a destination ski resort, lies in the heart of the Madison Range. The resort features 300 runs on four mountains connected by lifts. It spans 5,800 acres and boasts a 4,350-foot vertical drop.

LEFT: It's a mark of pride to lay down the first tracks after a nighttime snowfall, seen here on Evans Heaven, on a sunny powder morning at Whitefish Mountain Resort.

NEXT PAGES: Sunrise ignites 8,527-foot Ear Mountain, a recognizable landmark on the Rocky Mountain Front that was long a vision quest site for Native Americans.

FAR LEFT: Dusk brings on fairy-tale lighting over the village at Whitefish Mountain Resort. The ski area's longest run is 3.3 miles; its vertical drop is 2,353 feet.

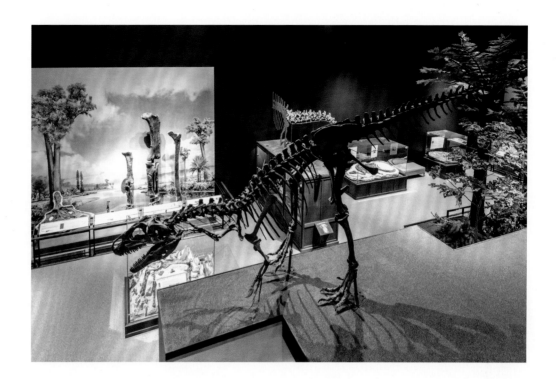

ABOVE: Dinosaur skeletons are among the highlights at the Museum of the Rockies, a Smithsonian Affiliate in Bozeman that features a planetarium, educational programs, and special exhibits.

LEFT: Autumn color accents the lower slopes of the Bridger Range, north of Bozeman. Mountain man Jim Bridger was an early trapper who guided settlers, explorers, miners, and even the U.S. Army through Montana in the mid-1800s.

BELOW: A pair of yellow-bellied marmots peek out of their rock burrow in the Lewis and Clark National Forest. Marmots utter a distinctive whistle that can be heard for a long distance.

RIGHT: The Powder River catches the day's last light in Custer County. Known for traditional cowboying, the rich bottom-lands along this 375-mile-long river support ranching and farming. This is the river referred to by the expression and song, "Powder River, Let 'er Buck!"

BELOW: Morning sunrise burns through the fog in the Upper Missouri River Breaks National Monument. The monument was designated in 2001 to protect the abundant and unique geological, cultural, and historical features along the Missouri River.

ABOVE: Bright pink monkeyflowers carpet the Hanging Gardens atop Logan Pass, in Glacier National Park. Its botanical name, ***Mimulus lewisii,*** honors Meriwether Lewis of the Lewis and Clark Expedition.

FACING PAGE: Drivers on Going-to-the-Sun Road in Glacier National Park sometimes need nerves of steel. The 50-mile-long road was completed in 1932 and features master masonry that utilized the native rocks.

Jesuit priests established the town of St. Ignatius in the 1850s, then built this church in the 1890s.
The church holds fifty-eight original paintings by Brother Joseph Carignano.

THESE PAGES: North American Indian Days on the Blackfeet Indian Reservation is held annually over four days during the second week of July. The Blackfoot Confederacy consists of four bands: the Blackfeet or Siksika, Blood or Kainai, and the Northern and Southern Piegan, also known as Pikuni or Piikani.

ABOVE: A grass dancer uses intricate step patterns that cause his elaborate costume to shimmy and fly around him.

TOP LEFT: A woman holds a cradle bedecked with skilled beadwork. Blackfeet beadwork commonly features geometric designs.

LEFT: The tiny tot dancing competition draws some serious—and seriously cute—competitors.

FAR LEFT: Tepees are a warm, traditional shelter and social gathering place for families during the event.

RIGHT: Kayakers take advantage of a calm day to paddle on Bowman Lake, a seven-mile-long glacier-carved lake in the mountainous northwestern corner of Glacier National Park.

BELOW: Lupine and Indian paintbrush carpet the forest floor. Paintbrush is a root hemiparasite, meaning it can connect to a host plant to get some of its water and nutrients.

ABOVE: Yellow warblers can be seen flitting through shrubs and trees along Montana's waterways. There are more than fifty species of warblers in North America; seasonally, Montana hosts thirty-two of them.

LEFT: The cheery yellow blossoms of arrowleaf balsamroot seem to lean toward the Mission Mountains from their perch in the National Bison Range near Moiese.

BELOW: Canola is a reliable crop in Montana, seen growing here in the Flathead Valley. The bright yellow flowers produce tiny seeds that can be pressed for cooking oil.

Migrating snow geese take off at sunrise at Freezout Lake Wildlife Management Area, a prairie pothole reserve along the Rocky Mountain Front.

LEFT: A white-tailed buck on high alert for does—and foes—during the autumn rut. This adaptable and strong deer species can be found from Canada to Peru.

FACING PAGE: The Swan Valley contains thousands of lakes, ponds, and wetlands that together create one of the richest, most intact wildlife habitats in the lower 48 states.

BELOW: The Yaak River in the Kootenai National Forest cascades over basement rock that is more than 800 million years old. Locals say the river's name is derived from the Kootenai Indian word *A'ak,* for arrow.

ABOVE: Snow geese take flight under a midday moon along the Rocky Mountain Front. Geese species that migrate through Montana include Canada, snow, greater white-fronted, Ross's, and cackling.

RIGHT: Shrubby penstemon blooms along the South Fork of the Flathead River, a designated National Wild and Scenic River renowned for its pristine wilderness characteristics.

BELOW: Red fox kits play outside their den in a field near Conrad. Montana has red foxes that sport white-tipped bushy tails and smaller swift foxes that have black-tipped tails.

LEFT: Youngsters take in the branding activity on the Hughes Ranch, near Stanford. Montana has more than 50,000 registered brands, each one a permanent mark of ownership.

FAR LEFT: A Black Angus bull rests near a timeworn old barn on ranchland at the base of the Chalk Buttes near Ekalaka. Montana ranchers raise more than 2.5 million cattle.

BELOW: This horse is so well trained it doesn't need a bridle, giving its cowboy a fine ride in the foothills of the Big Snowy Mountains near Judith Gap. Judith Gap is a low divide between the Musselshell and the Judith Rivers. Historically an Indian trail and a stagecoach route, the Gap now holds a productive wind farm.

LEFT: Beneath a gorgeous sunrise, Swiftcurrent Falls cascades through limestone formations in Glacier National Park. The park's geology is varied and visible; you can see direct evidence of uplift, erosion, deposition, thrust faults, a shallow sea, glaciation, and more.

NEXT PAGE: The 4th of July fireworks show over Whitefish Lake is an annual crowd-pleaser. The small town of Whitefish is known for its art galleries, live theater, museums, restaurants, and unparalleled four-season recreation.

BELOW: Fireweed is one of the first plants to colonize a burned area. Here, its flyaway seeds are ready to disperse.